DOT-TO-DOT FUN!

Count from 1 to 101

ARKADY ROYTMAN

D1412266

DOVER PUBLICATIONS
Garden City, New York

Counting from 1 to 101 is lots of fun! Connect the dots to reveal hidden pictures of dinosaurs and other prehistoric animals. Smile at a Smilodon (saber-toothed tiger), fly high with a Meganeura (giant dragonfly), and go for a swim with a Dunkleosteus (armored fish). Plus, you can color the finished drawings for even more fun! Complete solutions are included at the back of the book. The animals' names and the eras during which they lived are provided in the solutions section.

Note: The ★ symbol means that a number doesn't connect to the next number. Find the next number with a ★, and start connecting the dots again. For example, if there is a ★ beside number 40, pick up your pencil and begin again at number 41.

Bibliographical Note

Dinosaurs & Prehistoric Animals Dot-to-Dot Fun! is a new work,
first published by Dover Publications in 2023.

International Standard Book Number
ISBN-13: 978-0-486-85124-2
ISBN-10: 0-486-85124-9

Manufactured in the United States of America
85124901
www.doverpublications.com

1

★ Number **54** doesn't connect to number **55**.

★ Number **76** doesn't connect to number **77**.

★ Number **93** doesn't connect to number **94**.

★ Number **64** doesn't connect to number **65**.

★ Number **49** doesn't connect to number **50**.

7

★ Number **40** doesn't connect to number **41**.

Number **80** doesn't connect to number **81**.

★ Number **45** doesn't connect to number **46**.

★ Number **76** doesn't connect to number **77**.

★ Number **60** doesn't connect to number **61**.

★ Number **76** doesn't connect to number **77**.

★ Number **71** doesn't connect to number **72**.

★ Number **52** doesn't connect to number **53**.

★ Number **70** doesn't connect to number **71**.

20

★ Number **82** doesn't connect to number **83**.

★ Number **76** doesn't connect to number **77**.

★ Number **70** doesn't connect to number **71**.

★ Number **74** doesn't connect to number **75**.

★ Number **75** doesn't connect to number **76**.

★ Number **81** doesn't connect to number **82**.

★ Number **91** doesn't connect to number **92**.

★ Number **52** doesn't connect to number **53**.

★ Number **72** doesn't connect to number **73**.

★ Number **78** doesn't connect to number **79**.

★ Number **51** doesn't connect to number **52**.

SOLUTIONS

1. Allosaurus
Jurassic Period

2. Ankylosaurus
Cretaceous Period

3. Basilosaurus
Eocene Epoch

4. Baryonyx
Xiphactinus
Cretaceous Period

5. Brachiosaurus
Jurassic Period

6. Brontothere
Eocene Epoch

7. Carnotaurus
Cretaceous Period

8. Daeodon
Eocene Epoch

9. Dilophosaurus
Jurassic Period

10. Dreadnoughtus
Cretaceous Period

11. Dunkleosteus (armored fish)
Devonian Period

12. Giganotosaurus
Cretaceous Period

13. Helicoprion (saw shark)
Permian Period–Triassic Period

14. Ichthyosaurus
Jurassic Period

15. Iguanodon
Cretaceous Period

16. Mammuthus
(woolly mammoth)
Pliocene Epoch–Holocene Epoch

17. Megalodon
Miocene Epoch

18. Meganeura (giant dragonfly)
Arthropleura (giant millipede)
Carboniferous Period

19. Megatherium
(giant ground sloth)
Pleistocene Epoch

20. Microraptor
Cretaceous Period

21. Mosasaurus
Cretaceous Period

22. Ornithocheirus
Cretaceous Period

23. Pachycephalosaurus
Cretaceous Period

24. Parasaurolophus
Cretaceous Period

25. Phorusrhacid (terror bird)
Macrauchenia
Pleistocene Epoch

26. Plesiosaurus
Jurassic Period

27. Pteranodon
Cretaceous Period

28. Quetzalcoatlus
Cretaceous Period

29. Smilodon (saber-toothed tiger)
Glyptodon
Pleistocene Epoch

30. Spinosaurus
Sarcosuchus
Cretaceous Period

31. Stegosaurus
Dimorphodon
Jurassic Period

32. Stethacanthus (anvil shark)
Devonian Period

33. Styracosaurus
Cretaceous Period

34. Tapejara
Cretaceous Period

35. Therizinosaurus
Cretaceous Period

36. T. rex
Cretaceous Period

★ Number 51 doesn't connect to number 52.

37. Triceratops
Cretaceous Period

38. Velociraptor
Cretaceous Period